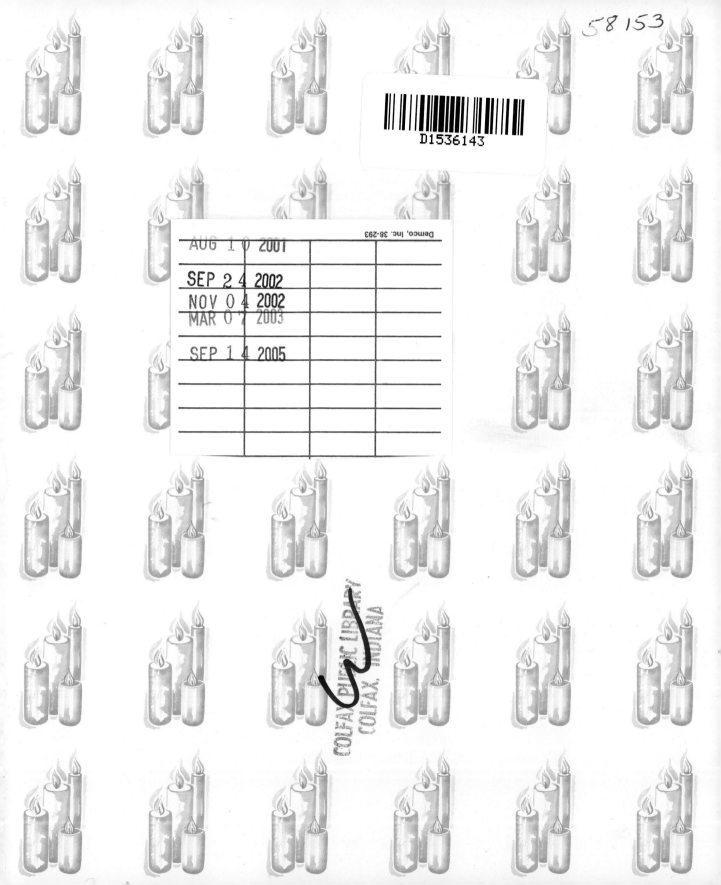

ínspirations

CANDLES

Over 20 projects for making and displaying candles

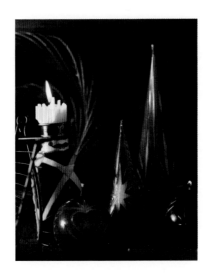

inspirations

CANDLES

Over 20 projects for making and displaying candles

DIANA CIVIL

PHOTOGRAPHY BY RUSSEL SADUR

LORENZ BOOKS

First published by Lorenz Books

Lorenz Books is an imprint of

Anness Publishing Limited

Hermes House

88-89 Blackfriars Road

London SE1 8HA

This edition published in the USA by Lorenz Books

Anness Publishing Inc., 27 West 20th Street, New York, NY 10011;

(800) 354-9657

Distributed in Canada by Raincoast Books

8680 Cambie Street, Vancouver, British Columbia V6P 6M9

ISBN 1-85967-448-8

Publisher: Joanna Lorenz

Senior Editor: Lindsay Porter

Photographer: Russel Sadur

Designer: Ian Sandom

Illustrators: Madeleine David and Lucinda Ganderton

Printed in Hong Kong/China

CONTENTS

INTRODUCTION

Candles have been going through something of a renaissance in recent years. No longer are we confined to red and green at Christmastime and plain white for the rest of the year. As a child, often the only candles in our house were the slightly shabby box of household candles pushed to the back of a cupboard, but kept on hand in case of emergencies. I still always have a box in my home because I particularly like their pure whiteness and simplicity and don't feel at all guilty about burning so many of them because they are so cheap. Today, tall, creamy church candles are a more elegant version of the humble household candle and will add elegance and glamour to any table setting.

In this book we aim to extend your enjoyment of candles by providing over 20 projects for making your own candles and candleholders. You can begin by simply painting or stencilling on plain candles to create your own personalized designs. If you would like to make your own from scratch you can choose to experiment with the traditional dipped method, or try your hand at using moulds or adding your own scents. To display your candles to best effect there are all kinds of shades and holders, from punched tin designs to an exquisite wire candle sconce. Go for Japanese minimalism with shades made of hand-made paper or recycle a galvanized steel bucket to make a container for the garden. Do remember that candles should not be left unattended. With proper care, you can enjoy each project in every area of the home.

Deborah Barker

CAST CANDLES

Candle moulds come in all shapes, sizes and materials, so it's not surprising that the range of possibilities available to both the amateur and professional candlemaker is endless. Generally, moulds are made of plastic, glass, rubber or metal and can be used over and over again.

YOU WILL NEED
moulds
primed wicks
wicking needles
mould sealer
measuring jug
scales
paraffin wax
stearin (10% of quantity of wax)
wax dye
kitchen knife
double boiler
wooden spoon
wax thermometer
ladle
scissors

1 Prepare each mould by threading a primed wick through the hole in the base. Tie the wick around the centre of a wicking needle to hold it firmly at the top of the mould.

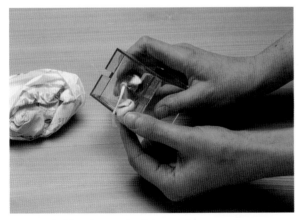

2 Pull the other end of the wick taut and press a large blob of mould sealer around it to prevent any leakage of wax through the hole.

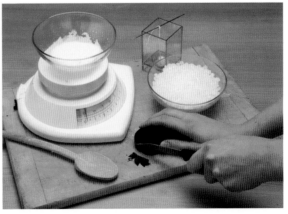

3 To calculate the amount of wax you will need, fill the mould with water and measure it. For every 100 ml/3½ fl oz water you will need 90 g/ 3½ oz cold wax. Weigh the wax and stearin and cut some wax dye from a dye disc.

4 Melt the stearin in a double boiler. Then add the dye and stir the two until they are completely melted. Add the wax to the double boiler and melt. Test the temperature with a thermometer. When the wax reaches 93°C/200°F turn off the heat.

5 Immediately ladle the wax into the prepared mould, taking care not to let it splash the sides. Tap the sides of the mould to release any trapped air bubbles.

6 As the wax sets, a slight dip will form around the wick. Prick the surface of the wax all over with a wicking needle.

7 Re-heat the remaining wax to 93°C/200°F and use to top up the mould.

8 Let the wax cool completely then remove the mould seal-er. The candle should slide out of the mould easily. Trim the wick.

SCENTED CANDLES

Scented candles create a delicious fragrance as they burn. You can use candle scents to impart a delicate rose fragrance to freshen a room or rich spicy fragrances to add a festive atmosphere. Aromatherapy oils can also be added to give your candles particular qualities.

YOU WILL NEED

scented wax dye, candle scents or
fruit-scented oil
spoon
rubber fruit mould
primed wick
mould sealer
wicking needle
measuring jug
scales
stearin (10% of quantity of wax)
double boiler
wooden spoon
paraffin wax
wax thermometer
card (cardboard)
scissors
glass bowl
ladle
assorted candle moulds

1 For the rubber mould candles, crush a small amount of wax dye into a paste with the back of a spoon. Thread a primed wick through the hole in the base and seal with a blob of mould sealer. Pull the wick taut and tie the opposite end around a wicking needle.

2 Calculate the amount of wax you will need by filling the mould with water. For every 100 ml/3½ fl oz water you will need 90 g/3½ oz cold wax. Place the stearin in the double boiler with the dye and any scent or oil and melt, stirring continually.

3 Add the wax and melt. Keep testing the temperature until the wax reaches 75°C/167°F. Turn off the heat.

4 Cut a circle out of the centre of the card (cardboard) to fit the neck of the mould, so that the rim rests comfortably on the card. Use the card mount to support the mould over a glass bowl. Carefully ladle the wax into the mould. Leave to set completely before removing the mould.

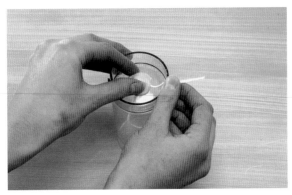

5 For the remaining candles, prepare the moulds by threading a primed wick through the hole in the base. Tie the wick around a wicking needle to hold it firmly at the top of the mould. Pull the other end of the wick so that it is taut and press a generous blob of mould sealer around it. Measure how much water the mould holds. For every 100 ml/3½ fl oz water you will need 90 g/3½ oz cold wax.

6 Melt the stearin, crush the dye and stir together. Add the wax to the double boiler and melt. Add a few drops of scent or oil if necessary and stir the mixture. When the melted wax reaches 93°C/200°F it is ready to ladle into the mould.

Above: A variety of these jolly candles will add a lighthearted note to a table centrepiece.

7 Carefully ladle the wax into the mould, leaving a gap of about 1 cm/½ in at the top. When the wax has settled for a couple of minutes tap the sides of the mould to get rid of any air bubbles. Let the candle cool, then re-heat the remaining wax and top up the mould. Let the wax cool completely then remove the candle from the mould.

DIPPED CANDLES

Tall, elegant dipped candles have a unique tapered shape that looks particularly stylish. A collection of dipped candles in assorted colours looks stunning simply hanging from a peg rail. A few nails hammered into a piece of board will serve as drying hooks for the candles.

YOU WILL NEED
paraffin wax
metal dipping can
large saucepan
wooden spoon
wax thermometer
wax dye
kitchen knife
primed wick, 60 cm/24 in for each pair of candles

1 Pour the paraffin wax into the dipping can and place the can in the saucepan. Pour water into the saucepan so that it comes about halfway up the side of the can. Heat the water to a gentle simmer and melt the wax, stirring occasionally. When the wax reaches a temperature of 70°C/158°F turn down the heat.

2 Cut up and crush your chosen wax dye and add to the wax, stirring until melted.

3 Hold a length of wick in the middle and dip the two ends into the wax so that approximately 5 cm/2 in on either side of your fingers remains uncovered. Dip the wick quickly and smoothly for a couple of seconds, then remove from the wax, ensuring that the two candles do not touch each other. The wax must be kept at a constant temperature of 70°C/158°F.

4 Hang up the pair of dipped wicks to cool for a couple of minutes, then repeat the dipping and setting process until the candles reach the thickness you require. This may take anything from 15 to 30 dips. Finally, to give the candles a smooth glossy top coat, increase the heat of the wax to 82°C/180°F. Quickly and smoothly dip the candles into the wax, remove and leave to cool. You may wish to trim the candle bases with a knife.

Above: You can create candy-twists from the basic dipped candles. See Techniques for the method.

SAND CANDLES

Sand candles are easy and fun to make. This technique allows you to create unusual shapes using all kinds of moulds, from shells and patty tins (pans) to decorative bowls and china. As the wax sets the sand sticks to it to form a decorative coating around the candle.

Bear in mind that the hotter the wax the more sand will adhere to the candle.

YOU WILL NEED
damp sand
large box lined with plastic
mould, such as a patty tin (pan) or shell
measuring jug
scales
stearin (10% of quantity of wax)
double boiler
wooden spoon
wax dye
kitchen knife
paraffin wax
wax thermometer
ladle
wicking needle
primed wick
scissors

1 Pour damp sand into the box and press to compact the sand. Push the mould into the sand firmly then remove it, leaving its imprint. See the Moulded Candles project to calculate the amount of wax needed. Heat the stearin in a double boiler, stirring while it melts. Cut the wax dye from the disc and add to the double boiler, then add the wax. Heat until it reaches 82°C/180°F. Ladle the wax into the mould.

2 Leave the wax to harden. Re-heat the remaining wax and top up the dip in the centre of the candle. Leave the wax until just set enough to hold a wick in place.

3 Push a wicking needle into the centre of the candle to make a hole and lower the wick into it. When the wax is fully dry, remove the candle from the sand and trim the wick.

4 Pour damp sand into the box and press down firmly. Push a shell into the sand, press down firmly and remove carefully to leave an imprint.

5 Ladle wax into the mould and insert a wick as in steps 2 and 3 to create the candle.

Left: A selection of small candles displayed in a box of sand is a delightful evocation of the seaside.

CARVED CANDLES

Plain candles can be dipped in a richly coloured outer coating, then carved using a simple tool to create candles with a distinct folk-art flavour. The carving shows off the plain creamy-white wax underneath the colourful coating, and patterns can be as simple or as decorative as you choose.

YOU WILL NEED
linoleum-cutting tool or bradawl
selection of uncoloured candles with
dipped outer coatings
pencil (optional)
paintbrush

1 With the cutting tool, mark a line from the bottom of the candle to the wick. The cut line should be deep enough to see the natural wax underneath the coloured surface. If you are unsure about cutting your design freehand, lightly mark each line with a pencil before cutting.

2 Cut three more lines down the candle, dividing it into quarters. Cut small feathery lines branching off the first line at regular intervals from the base of the candle to the wick. Repeat the feathered design on the other three sides. Use a paintbrush to brush away the excess wax shavings as you work.

3 In each of the panels between the feathered lines, lightly mark out a heart shape. Once you are happy with the shape, score and cut deeply to reach the uncoloured wax beneath the surface colour.

4 In the centre of the heart, mark out a small star shape, and cut a fan of five straight lines over each heart. Repeat the design around the candle.

5 On the top of the candle, in between the feathered lines, mark out four matching stars and cut out neatly.

6 A conical candle looks stylish with a series of feathery lines branching from one main stem.

7 A standard pillar candle can be transformed with a simple star design.

8 Decorate a spherical candle with four feathered lines and a star in each panel.

Left: Folk-art motifs complement this fat pillar candle. A V-shaped linoleum cutting tool will allow you to make designs with precision.

EMBOSSED CANDLES

Corrugated cardboard can be turned into an unusual candle mould: you can experiment with a variety of different-sized ridges and textures to complete a decorative array of candles. Natural-coloured wax gives these textured candles a contemporary and stylish look.

YOU WILL NEED
corrugated cardboard
craft knife
metal ruler
plant spray
strong tape
plastic container lid
bradawl
primed wick
mould sealer
wicking needle
stearin (10% of quantity of wax)
double boiler
wax dye
kitchen knife
wooden spoon
paraffin wax
wax thermometer
ladle
scissors

1 Cut a rectangle of corrugated cardboard to the desired size of the candle: the length of the card will determine the circumference of the candle and the width will correspond to the height. Spray the cardboard thoroughly with water, then roll it into a cylinder and join and cover the sides with strong tape.

2 Pierce the middle of a plastic container lid with a bradawl and thread a primed wick through the hole. Stand the cardboard roll centrally over the lid. Seal all around the base of the roll with mould sealer to ensure the mould is watertight. Wind the other end of the wick around a wicking needle and rest it across the top of the cardboard. Seal the hole under the base of the plastic lid with mould sealer to make it watertight. ▶

3 Melt the stearin in a double boiler. Cut off the quantity of wax dye required. Stir until melted. Add the wax to the mixture and heat until the mixture reaches 82°C/180°F. Ladle the molten wax into the mould.

4 Leave the wax to cool. A dip will form in the centre of the candle surface. Top up with more molten wax and leave to cool completely.

5 Carefully remove the candle from the plastic lid by pulling away the mould sealer. Using a craft knife, cut through the tape down the side of the mould.

6 Remove the tape and finally peel off the cardboard from around the candle. Trim the wick.

Right: These embossed candles are complemented by a natural-coloured box and make a stylish gift.

HAND-MADE FLOATING CANDLES

Small floating rose candles make a charming centrepiece and a highly romantic decoration for a dinner table. Float them in a glass bowl or vase so that the candlelight reflects around the room. Alternatively, single candles could be placed in individual glasses.

YOU WILL NEED
stearin (10% of quantity of wax)
double boiler
wax dye
kitchen knife
wooden spoon
paraffin wax
wax thermometer
baking tray
greaseproof paper
ladle
wooden board
primed wick

1 Melt the stearin in a double boiler and add the wax dye, cutting off the quantity required with a kitchen knife. Stir until melted. Add the paraffin wax and heat until the mixture reaches a temperature of 82°C/180°F. Line a baking tray with a sheet of greaseproof paper and ladle the mixture into the tray in an even layer. While the wax is still warm, peel away the greaseproof paper and place the wax sheet on to a wooden board.

2 Using a kitchen knife roughly cut petal shapes out of the wax.

3 Working quickly, take the first petal shape and roll it around a piece of primed wick, leaving about 2 cm/¾ in of the wick protruding above the top of the petal.

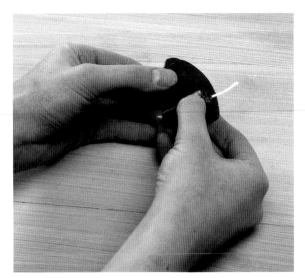

4 Take another petal and quickly wrap this one around the first, overlapping the edges. You need to work quickly before the wax hardens and becomes too brittle to mould without cracking. If this happens, re-melt the wax and start again.

5 Continue to build up the layers of petals, adding five or six petals to create the finished rose shape. Repeat until you have the required number of roses.

MOSAIC CANDLE POTS

Inexpensive tumblers make ideal candle pots and can be transformed into works of art by sponging on patterns in rich jewel colours. You need not use matching glassware: a variety of junk-shop finds or even jam jars in an array of shapes and sizes will create the right overall effect.

YOU WILL NEED
craft knife and cutting mat
small pieces of compacted foam rubber
(children's sponge alphabet shapes are ideal)
glass tumblers
ceramic paints in several colours, including gold
plate for mixing paints
fine paintbrush
measuring jug
scales
paraffin wax
stearin (10% of quantity of wax)
wax dye
kitchen knife
primed wick
scissors
wicking needles
double boiler
wooden spoon
wax thermometer
ladle
gold lustre paint

1 Using the craft knife and cutting mat, carefully cut the compacted foam rubber into small, equal-sized squares.

2 Clean the tumblers thoroughly and leave to dry. Tip a small quantity of ceramic paint in each colour on to a plate. Carefully holding a sponge square, dip the surface into the paint and, starting at the base of the first tumbler, firmly apply the painted surface to the glass. Repeat this process, alternating the colours around the tumbler, until it is completely decorated. Continue with the remaining tumblers. Leave to dry thoroughly.

3 Using a fine paintbrush and a little gold ceramic paint, decorate the rim of each tumbler and leave to dry. Calculate the amount of wax needed to fill your tumblers by filling them with water and measuring it. For every 100 ml/3½ fl oz water you will need 90 g/3½ oz cold wax.

4 Weigh out the required amount of wax and stearin and select a wax dye. Cut off enough wax dye from a disc to give the depth of colour required.

5 For each tumbler, tie a length of primed wick around a wicking needle, pull it taut and place a wick in each tumbler so that it hangs in the centre and just reaches the bottom.

6 Melt the stearin in the double boiler. Then add the dye, breaking up the pieces and stirring them in until completely melted. Add the wax to the double boiler.

7 Use a thermometer to test the temperature of the melted wax. When it reaches 93°C/ 200°F, ladle it into the centre of each candle pot, ensuring that the wax does not splash on to the sides. Tap the sides of the tumblers to release any air bubbles. As the wax cools, a slight dip will form around the wick. Prick the surface of the dipped area all over with a wicking needle and top up the candle with more melted wax.

8 Allow the wax to set. Use a small brush or your finger to cover lightly the top of each candle with gold lustre paint to add a rich, glistening sheen to the finished candle pots.

SHELL CANDLES

Shells are wonderfully decorative natural containers for wax, and a group of shells in different shapes and sizes creates a stylish and dramatic display. Ensure the shells are completely clean and dry before you use them.

YOU WILL NEED
selection of shells
mould sealer
measuring jug
scales
paraffin wax
stearin (10% of quantity of wax)
wax dye
kitchen knife
primed wick
scissors
wick sustainers
double boiler
wooden spoon
wax thermometer
ladle
wicking needle
lustre paint in gold and silver
plate for mixing paints

1 Place the shells on a flat surface and stick them down with small blobs of mould sealer if necessary to stop them wobbling. Using mould sealer, block up any holes or cracks in the shells to prevent the wax from leaking.

2 To calculate the amount of wax you will need, fill the shells with water and measure it. For every 100 ml/3½ fl oz water you should use 90 g/3½ oz cold paraffin wax. Weigh out the wax and stearin. Cut enough wax dye from a disc to give the depth of colour you want and crush it.

3 Cut a length of wick for each shell. Large shells can have a length of wick supported in their centres before the wax is added by securing a primed wick with a wick sustainer. With smaller shells it is easier to add a piece of primed wick once the wax has been added.

4 Melt the stearin in the double boiler. Then add the dye, stirring until completely melted. Add the paraffin wax to the double boiler and melt.

5 Test the temperature with a thermometer. The molten wax is ready when it reaches a temperature of 93°C/200°F.

6 Using a ladle, carefully pour the molten wax into the moulds.

7 For the small shells, leave the wax until it is set just enough to hold the wicks in place. Position short lengths of primed wick in the centre of each wax-filled shell, making the hole using a wicking needle. Leave a short piece of wick extending above the wax. As the wax shrinks, top up with more molten wax and leave to cool.

8 Place small amounts of gold and silver lustre paint on a plate and, using your finger, lightly rub the paint on to the surface of the candles to create a decorative sheen.

HAND-PAINTED CHURCH CANDLES

For special occasions, give plain candles a personalized touch by decorating them yourself. You can embellish candles of any shape or size and you don't need to be experienced with a paintbrush or an expert artist, as long as you have a steady hand.

YOU WILL NEED
acetate or stencil card (cardboard)
felt-tip pen
craft knife and cutting mat
plain candles
masking tape
stencil brush
poster paints in gold, silver and black
scrap paper
tracing paper
pencil
paintbrushes
gold size
Dutch gold leaf
tape measure
carbon paper

1 For the stencilled candle, mark out your chosen design on to acetate or stencil card (cardboard) with a felt-tip pen or, if you prefer, trace a motif from a card or wrapping paper. Using a craft knife and cutting mat carefully cut out the stencil.

2 Attach the stencil to the candle using masking tape. Dab the stencil brush in a little poster paint and remove any excess on a piece of scrap paper. Apply the paint through the stencil using a firm, even pressure, then remove the stencil and reposition on the candle.

3 For the gilded candle, draw a design on tracing paper. Tape the drawing around the candle, and draw over the outline of the design using a pencil: this should leave a faint impression in the wax. Remove the drawing and, using a fine paintbrush and the gold size, paint over all the areas to be gilded.

4 When the size is tacky, roll the candle on to a sheet of Dutch gold leaf, which will stick to the painted areas. If your sheets of gold leaf are smaller than the candle, work on one area at a time until the candle is completed.

5 For the hand-painted candle, measure the height and circumference of the candle and transfer these dimensions to a sheet of tracing paper. Trace a cherub design on to the tracing paper, or draw your own design. Position the tracing over a sheet of carbon paper (ink-side down) on the candle and stick in position using masking tape.

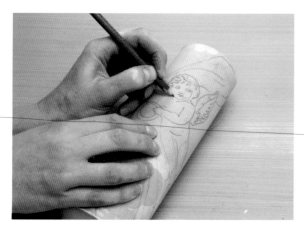

6 Using a pencil, draw over the outlines of the pattern to transfer it to the surface of the candle. Carefully peel back the tracing and carbon paper to check that the whole pattern has been successfully transferred. If necessary, replace the paper and go over any missing parts again.

7 Using a fine paintbrush, fill in the areas of the design with poster paints. Here, the entire design was painted in gold, with highlights added using silver.

8 To add depth and shading to the design, paint in shadows using black. This will instantly add a three-dimensional finish to your design.

FLOATING FISH CANDLES

Candles look good floating in water in all types of containers, from wonderfully ornate coloured glass dishes to the most basic jars placed at ground level in the garden. These fish candles add a quirky touch displayed in a bowl.

YOU WILL NEED
craft knife and cutting mat
metal ruler
piece of card (cardboard) 30 x 22.5 cm/12 x 9 in
masking tape
baking tray
greaseproof paper
mould sealer
stearin (10% of quantity of wax)
double boiler
wax dye
wooden spoon
paraffin wax
wax thermometer
ladle
scissors

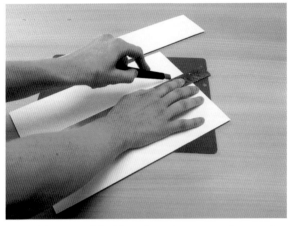

1 Using a craft knife and cutting mat and a metal ruler, cut the card (cardboard) into three strips measuring 30 x 7.5 cm/12 x 3 in.

2 Mark a line across the centre of each 30 cm/12 in strip. Using the craft knife and metal ruler, lightly score along this line. This will enable the card to be folded without creasing.

3 Measure in 3 cm/1¼ in from each end of each strip of card, mark and lightly score a line as before. Turn the strip over and measure in a further 3 cm/1¼ in and repeat. Fold the strip into a fish shape along the scored lines, curving the sides. Stick the ends of the template together using masking tape. ▶

4 Line a baking tray with a sheet of greaseproof paper. Position the fish moulds on the grease-proof paper and press mould sealer around the outside to prevent any wax from leaking out through the bottom of the moulds.

5 Melt the stearin in the top of the double boiler and add the dye, stirring until thoroughly blend-ed, then add the paraffin wax. Heat until the wax reaches a temperature of 82°C/180°F.

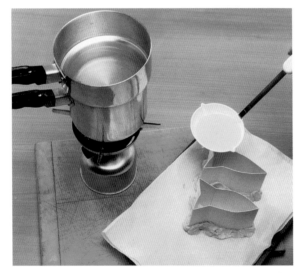

6 Carefully ladle small amounts of wax into the fish moulds and gently tap the sides to release any air bubbles. When the wax has started to set, re-heat the remaining wax and top up each candle.

7 Cut pieces of primed wick to the length required. While the wax is still soft but firm enough to hold the wick upright, push a length of wick into each candle. Leave until completely set, then carefully push the candles out of the moulds.

CANDLES IN TIN CANS

Nothing is more satisfying than recycling a throwaway item into something original and decorative. Tin cans are wonderful ready-made containers for candles and old cheese graters are both unusual and effective.

YOU WILL NEED
selection of tin cans
measuring jug
stearin (10% of quantity of wax)
scales
double boiler
wooden spoon
paraffin wax
beeswax
wax thermometer
ladle
wicking needle
primed container wick (special wick
that stays lit in molten wax)
pillar candle mould
primed wick
mould sealer
wax dye
kitchen knife
scissors
selection of cheese graters

1 Fill the cans with water and pour this into a jug to determine the quantity of wax to use. For each 100 ml/3½ fl oz water you will need to use 90 g/ 3½ oz cold wax. Melt the stearin in the double boiler, stirring until melted.

2 Add the wax to the double boiler. A mixture of 50% paraffin wax and 50% beeswax will give the wax a soft natural yellow colour and lengthen the burning time of the candles. Melt the wax. Test the temperature of the liquid wax and remove from the heat when it reaches 82°C/180°F.

▶

3 Using a ladle, carefully fill the cans with the molten wax to just below the rim. When the wax is nearly set, make a hole through the centre of each candle with a wicking needle and insert a piece of primed container wick in each tin. Pour in more molten wax to top up each container as necessary.

4 To calculate the amount of wax you will need for a pillar candle fill the mould with water and measure it - for every 100 ml/3½ fl oz water you will need 90 g/3½ oz cold paraffin wax. Thread a primed wick through the hole in the base of the mould and press a blob of mould sealer around it.

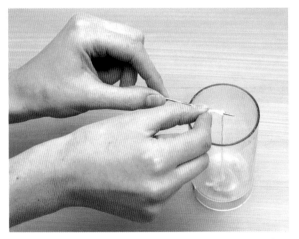

5 Pull the wick so that it is taut and tie it around the middle of a wicking needle to hold it firmly at the top of the mould. Cut enough wax dye from a disc to give the depth of colour you want and crush it.

6 Melt the stearin in the double boiler then add the dye, stirring until melted. Add the wax and heat to 93°C/200°F, then ladle into the centre of the mould, leaving a gap of 1 cm/½ in at the top. Leave the wax to settle and start to set, then top up the candle with more molten wax. When the wax is completely hard, remove the candle from the mould and trim the wick. Repeat, and then place the finished candles inside the cheese graters.

PILLAR WITH LEAVES

Pillar candles can be decorated in a variety of ways to transform them from the ordinary into works of art. This pillar candle is richly encrusted with leaves, simply cut from sheets of warm wax using a pastry (cookie) cutter.

YOU WILL NEED
straight-sided glass tumbler or
pillar candle mould
measuring jug
scales
paraffin wax
stearin (10% of quantity of wax)
wax dyes
kitchen knife
double boiler
wooden spoon
wax thermometer
primed wick
wick sustainer (optional)
wicking needle
mould sealer (optional)
pine candle scent (optional)
ladle
baking tray
greaseproof paper
circular fluted pastry (cookie) cutter
picture framer's wax gilt
wax glue

1 Fill the tumbler or candle mould with water and measure it – for every 100 ml/3½ fl oz water you will need 90 g/3½ oz cold paraffin wax. Weigh out the wax and stearin. Cut enough wax dye from a disc to give the depth of colour you want and crush it.

2 Melt the stearin in the double boiler. Add the dye, stirring until it is completely melted. Add the wax to the boiler and melt. While the wax is melting, prepare the mould as in Step 3. When the wax reaches a temperature of 93°C/200°F it is ready to pour into the mould.

3 To prepare the mould, thread a primed wick on to a wick sustainer and place in the centre of the base of the tumbler. (If you are using a candle mould, thread the wick through the hole in the base and seal with mould sealer.) Pull the wick taut and tie the other end around a wicking needle to hold it firmly at the top of the glass or mould.

4 To add a fragrance to the wax, pour a few drops of pine candle scent into the wax mixture and stir gently to combine thoroughly.

5 Ladle the wax into the centre of the mould, taking care not to let it splash on to the sides. Leave a gap of about 1 cm/$\frac{1}{2}$ in at the top of the mould. When the wax has settled for a couple of minutes, tap the side of the mould to get rid of any trapped air bubbles. Leave the candle to set, then remove from the mould.

6 Line the baking tray with a sheet of greaseproof paper. Melt another small batch of the wax mixture and slowly pour it into the tray to form an even slab of wax about 5 mm/$\frac{1}{4}$ in thick.

7 When the wax is nearly set, use the pastry (cookie) cutter to cut out 8-10 wax leaves. Bend the leaves gently around the handle of a wooden spoon. If the wax becomes too hard, peel it off the greaseproof paper, re-melt and repeat the procedure. Make two more batches of leaves, using pale green and ivory wax.

8 Score veins on each of the leaves and rub over lightly using your fingertip and the wax gilt.

9 Melt some wax glue in the double boiler. Apply a small dab of glue to each leaf and stick them around the base of the candle, alternating the colours.

10 Continue building up the leaves around the base until you are happy with the arrangement. For added lustre, apply a little of the wax gilt to the surface of the candle.

TWISTED WIRE CANDELABRA

Copper wire is easy to bend and mould and is therefore ideal for making a twisted candleholder as it can be as simple or as ornate as you choose. It's a good idea to work out a rough design for your candleholder on paper before you begin to cut or twist any wire.

YOU WILL NEED
hacksaw
heavy-gauge copper wire
tape measure
felt-tip pen
pliers
spray paint can or similar
broom handle or similar
beeswax sheets
primed wick
scissors

1 Using the hacksaw, cut three pieces of copper wire 91 cm/36 in long.

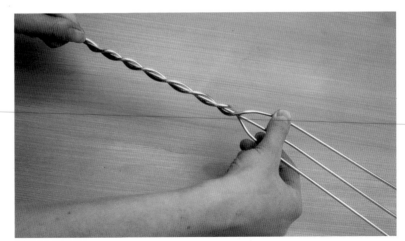

2 Use a felt-tip pen to mark each length of wire 30 cm/12 in and 56 cm/22 in from one end. Hold the three wires together and, keeping the central wire straight, twist the other two strands around it between the two marked points. You should be able to do this using your hands, but it may help to use a pair of pliers on thicker gauge wire. ▶

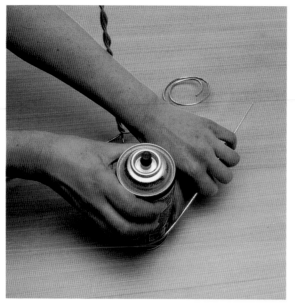

3 At the bottom of the candelabra (with the longer sections of untwisted wires) bend the centre of one piece into a circular shape around a spray paint can or similar object.

4 Using a pair of pliers, continue to bend the end of the wire around inside the circle to make smaller concentric circles until all the wire has been used up. Repeat to make the other two feet.

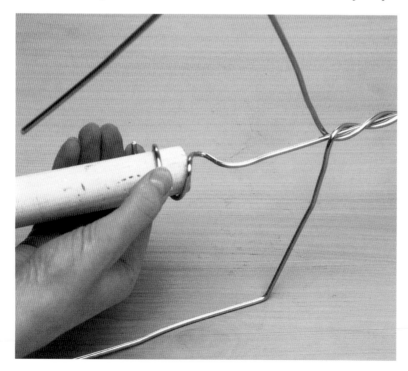

5 At the top of the candelabra, beginning with the central wire, twist the end around a wooden mould – such as a broom handle – that is the same thickness as the candles you intend to use. Work two or three twists into the wire, then ensure that the rest of the wire above the twisted section is vertically in line with it.

6 To shape the two outer pieces of wire, use the pliers to bend them up into a vertical position approximately 10 cm/4 in from the top of the twisted section of the candelabra.

7 Use the broom handle to twist the ends of the outer wires into circles to hold the candles. Neaten all three candle-holding sections with pliers.

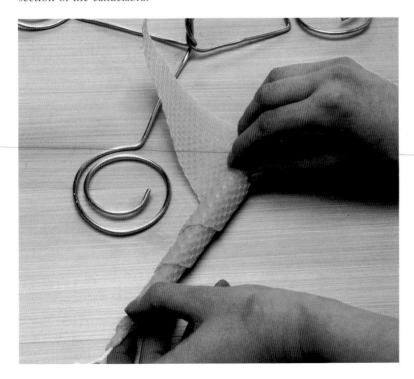

8 Stand up the candelabra and position the feet to provide a stable base. To make the candles, roll triangular sheets of beeswax around lengths of primed wick and place one in each of the three holders. Trim the wicks to length.

PUNCHED TIN CANDLEHOLDERS

Simple patterns punched into even the most basic of tin cans make very pretty candleholders. To prevent the cans from denting when the patterns are punched you need to line it with a solid material, and wax is an excellent medium for this purpose. When you have completed the design, melt the wax to remove it from the can.

YOU WILL NEED
tin cans
can opener
tape measure
tracing paper
pencil
scissors
measuring jug
scales
stearin (10% of quantity of wax)
paraffin wax
double boiler
wooden spoon
wax thermometer
masking tape
punch
hammer
bucket

1 Soak the labels off the cans. Open the cans with a can opener and discard the lids. Remove the contents and wash and dry the cans thoroughly.

2 Measure the height and circumference of each can. Cut out pieces of tracing paper to fit these measurements.

3 For each design, fold the tracing paper in half widthways and draw a pattern on one half.

4 Turn the folded paper over and trace the second half of the pattern. Unfold the paper and redraw any faint lines.

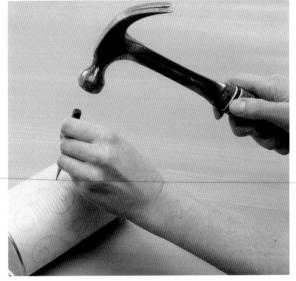

5 Fill each can with water and measure it. For every 100 ml/3½ fl oz water you will need 90 g/ 3½ oz cold paraffin wax. Melt the stearin and wax in a double boiler. When the wax reaches a temperature of 82°C/180°F pour into the cans and leave to set.

6 When the wax is cold and hard, place a template around each can and fix in position with masking tape. Using a punch and hammer, gently but firmly punch out the pattern on the can following the template. The wax will ensure that the can stays in shape and the holes are of equal size.

7 When the entire pattern has been punched out, remove the tracing paper. Invert each can in a bucket and pour boiling water over it. This will soften the candle so that it slips out easily. Rinse each can with boiling water to remove any traces of wax.

8 Remove the remaining ends of the cans with a can opener.

DRIED-FLOWER CANDLES

All kinds of natural materials can be used to decorate candles, from fresh petals and leaves to dried spices and fruits. Dried fruit slices such as apples or oranges are particularly attractive when arranged around the sides of a candle scented with the same fragrance.

YOU WILL NEED
pillar candle mould
measuring jug
scales
paraffin wax
stearin (10% of quantity of wax)
primed wick
wicking needle
mould sealer
double boiler
wax dye
kitchen knife
wooden spoon
wax thermometer
ladle
wax glue
glue brush
dried flower petals and leaves
baking tray
greaseproof paper
artificial gold berries and leaves (optional)

1 To calculate the amount of wax you will need, fill the mould with water and measure it. For every 100 ml/3½ fl oz water you will need 90 g/3½ oz cold paraffin wax. Weigh out the wax and stearin.

2 Prepare the mould by threading a primed wick through the hole in the base. Tie the wick around a wicking needle to hold it firmly at the top of the mould. Then pull the other end of the wick taut and press a blob of mould sealer around it to prevent any leakage of wax.

3 Melt the stearin in the double boiler. Then add the dye, breaking the disc into pieces with a kitchen knife and stirring them in until dissolved.

4 Add the wax to the double boiler and melt. Test the temperature using a wax thermometer.

5 When the wax reaches 93°C/200°F, ladle it into the mould, taking care not to let the wax splash on to the sides. Tap the sides of the mould to release any air bubbles. Allow the wax to cool, when a slight dip will form around the wick. Top up with more molten wax and leave to set. Remove the candle from the mould.

6 Melt a little wax glue and use it to fix the petals and foliage around the candle. Leave to set.

▶

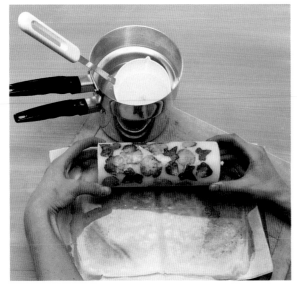

7 Melt a little more of the paraffin wax mixture and pour into a baking tray lined with grease-proof paper. As soon as the wax has spread over the tray, carefully roll the candle in the wax to form a coating over the petals and leaves. Leave to set.

8 As an alternative decoration for a festive occasion, apply gold leaves and berries to the candle in the same way.

GALVANIZED BUCKET AND FRAME

Galvanized buckets can be bought very cheaply from hardware stores or florists' and are ideal for filling with wax to make candle pots for outdoor use. Use them to line a path or walkway, light up a patio or brighten a herbaceous border.

YOU WILL NEED
hacksaw
heavy-gauge galvanized wire
florists' wire
flux
blow-torch
safety goggles and protective gloves
solder
pliers
chain
S-hook
small galvanized bucket
car spray paints in brown, green, gold
and white
measuring jug
scales
primed wick
2 wooden spoons
stearin (10% of quantity of wax)
double boiler
wax dye
kitchen knife
paraffin wax
citronella candle scent
wax thermometer
ladle

1 Using the hacksaw, cut two pieces of galvanized wire 112 cm/44 in long. Bend one into a circle.

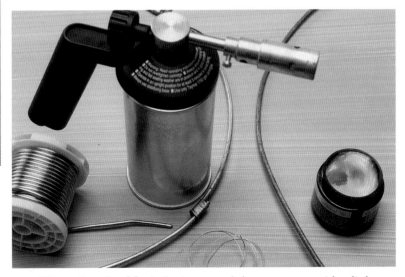

2 Wrap a length of florists' wire around the seam, coat with a little flux, then, wearing safety goggles and protective gloves, hold the blow-torch and solder over the seam, applying the heat for a few minutes. ▶

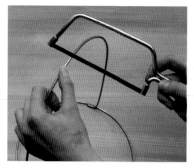

3 Bend the remaining piece of wire into a curve to make an arch to attach to each side of the wire circle. Using pliers, bend 1 cm/½ in at each end at right angles to the rest. Bend the ends in opposite directions to add strength to the arch. Wire and solder both ends to the circular base as before.

4 At the centre of the arch, make a small nick in the wire using a hacksaw, and attach a short piece of chain and an S-hook. Close the top loop of the S-hook with the pliers.

5 Spray the galvanized bucket lightly with paint, using a mixture of the four colours. The result should be a soft subtle mist of colour to create the effect of a verdigris finish.

6 See the Moulded Candles project to calculate the amount of cold wax needed. Prepare the bucket by tying a primed wick around a wooden spoon. Pull the other end so that the wick is taut and place it in the centre of the bucket.

7 Melt the stearin in the double boiler. Then add the dye as required, breaking the disc into pieces with a kitchen knife and stirring until completely melted. Add the paraffin wax to the double boiler and melt. Add a few drops of citronella candle scent to the mixture. When the melted wax reaches 93°C/200°F, ladle it into the bucket, leaving a gap of about 1 cm/ ½ in at the top. Tap the sides of the bucket to get rid of any air bubbles. As the wax cools a slight dip will form around the wick. Carefully top up the container with more melted wax. Leave to set completely, then suspend the container from the S-hook on the frame.

FOIL-DECORATED CANDLES

For festive occasions you can turn plain-coloured candles into jewel-encrusted fantasies. The fine gold foil from chocolate wrappers, cut into delicate shapes, resembles gold leaf when applied to the surface of the candle in this way.

YOU WILL NEED
gold foil
craft knife and cutting mat
metal ruler
pencil
small, sharp scissors
spherical and pillar candles
bodkin
candle for heating bodkin
assortment of small beads and sequins
dressmakers' pins
strong clear glue
small flat-backed plastic "jewels"

1 Use your fingers to flatten the creases out of the gold foil and cut out long strips about 3 mm/ ⅛ in wide using a craft knife and cutting mat and a metal ruler.

2 Cut out 4 cm/1½ in squares from the foil, fold each one into eight and trace out a star design using a pencil.

3 Using a craft knife or small, sharp scissors, cut out the motif and then open out carefully.

▶

6 5

4 Place the foil star on the candle, then heat a bodkin in a candle flame for a few seconds. Run the point of the bodkin over the foil to melt the wax underneath and fuse the foil to the candle.

5 Place the foil strips one at a time in position on the candle, forming a criss-cross pattern around the star motifs. Use the heated bodkin again to fix the strips in place.

6 Pick up a small bead on a dressmakers' pin, then a sequin. Heat the pin briefly in the candle flame and push it into the candle at a point where the foil strips cross. Repeat at all the crossing-points.

7 Glue flat-backed plastic "jewels" in the centre of each star shape. Repeat the decorations with the remaining candles.

WIRE CANDLE SCONCE

Delicate coils of pale galvanized wire make an ornate candleholder to hang on the wall. The template is simple to follow if you first enlarge it to the actual size of the sconce, then lay the coils over it as you bend them to check that they match.

YOU WILL NEED
paper
pencil
wire-cutters
2 mm/⅛ in gauge galvanized wire
tape measure
long-nosed pliers
fine galvanized wire
clear adhesive tape
candle

1 Scale up the template at the back of the book to the actual finished size and draw it on a piece of paper. Using wire-cutters, cut the 2 mm/⅛ in wire into the following lengths: 2 x 30 cm/12 in for the top hanger and lower coils; 1 x 50 cm/20 in for the centre piece; 4 x 55 cm/21½ in for the side pieces; 1 x 80 cm/32 in for the candleholder.

2 Using the long-nosed pliers, bend each length to fit the relevant coiled shape on the sconce design.

3 Take the top hanger piece and wind the fine wire around the crossover point, trim the wire and take the ends to the back of the sconce.

4 Turn the shape over and twist the ends of the fine wire together securely, then snip off any excess. Wire all the seams in this way.

5 Secure two of the side pieces in position under the hanger with small tabs of adhesive tape at the points indicated. The tape will hold the coils steady while you make the wire seams.

6 Make strong wire seams at the taped points using fine wire.

7 Tape the centre piece into position between the two side pieces, then wind the fine wire around the small triangular shape in the centre.

8 Tape the other pieces into position and make small wire seams to secure them, winding a short piece of fine wire around three times. Secure the ends by twisting them together at the back.

9 Make the candleholder with the remaining length of 2 mm/⅛ in wire. Begin with a small spiral, then wind the wire around the candle about five times.

10 Bend the end of the wire underneath the coil across the base (the base of the candle will rest on this), and then into an elongated hook shape at the back. Hook the holder on to the sconce and wire securely in place.

ROPE CANDLESTICKS

These chunky candlesticks have a solid, sculptural quality. Rough coils of natural jute rope provide a strong, satisfying contrast in texture with smooth, creamy candles. The base can be made from several layers of cardboard instead of fibreboard.

YOU WILL NEED
pencil
paper
9 mm/½ in sheet medium density fibreboard (MDF)
jigsaw
wood saw
tape measure
wooden broom handle
hot glue gun and glue sticks
jute rope
7 cm/2¾ in diameter terracotta plant pot saucers
small screws
hammer
screwdriver
scissors

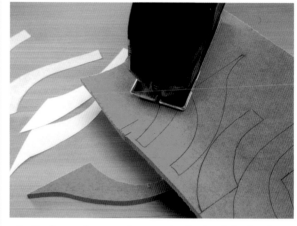

1 Scale up the templates at the back of the book and draw the "leg" and "arm" shapes on a sheet of MDF. Use a jigsaw to cut out the shapes.

2 Use a wood saw to cut a 20 cm/8 in length from the broom handle for the central shaft. Using a glue gun, squeeze a small amount of glue on to one end of the shaft, wind the end of a length of jute rope into a small spiral and press on to the glue.

3 Squeeze a few lines of glue along the shaft for about 5 cm/2 in and wind the rope tightly around it. Working in 5 cm/2 in sections, continue in this way until the shaft is completely covered with rope. Finish with a small spiral at the other end of the shaft, as before.

4 Take two terracotta saucers and turn them upside-down. Using a small screw and a hammer, gently tap a hole through the centre of each saucer.

5 Glue a saucer to the top of each candlestick arm, then screw in place.

6 Wrap each arm with rope, using the glue gun as before. At the edge of the saucer, fray and flatten out the end of the rope and glue in place, then glue and wind on the rope in close spiral rows, covering the frayed end neatly. Continue down the arm, stopping at the end of the inner curve. Do not trim off the end of the rope.

7 Glue the arm to the shaft of the candlestick, then glue the rope along both sides of the seam where the arm meets the shaft.

8 To cover the remainder of the arm, glue the rope in concentric rows forming a triangular pattern as shown. Attach the other arm in the same way.

9 Cover the centre with a spiral of rope, working from the outside to the centre.

10 Glue the three legs, evenly spaced, around the base of the candlestick shaft. Cover with rope, beginning at the foot and working up towards the seam. Cover the seam with a concentric triangular pattern as before.

JAPANESE PAPER LANTERNS

The subtle textural variations of handmade Japanese paper are shown to perfection in these beautiful candle shades. Their restrained, organic forms have an oriental feel in keeping with the material.

YOU WILL NEED
paper
pencil
sheets of hand-made Japanese paper
scissors
masking tape
bradawl
thin willow twig
double-sided tape
craft knife and cutting mat
natural pine strip (used in basket-making) or
thin card (cardboard)

1 For the simple shade, scale up the template at the back of the book and draw the lantern shape on the Japanese paper. Make faint pencil marks to indicate the positions of the holes for the fastener. Cut out the shade.

2 Place a small tab of masking tape on the back of the paper at each hole position, to act as a reinforcement.

3 Using the bradawl, pierce small holes where indicated on the template.

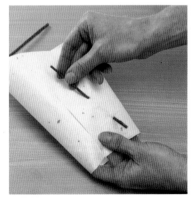

4 Cut a short length of willow twig to act as a fastener, then bend the lantern into a cylinder and match up the holes. Insert the twig to hold the lantern in shape. ▶

5 For the petal shade, scale up the template at the back of the book and draw the shapes on the Japanese paper. Cut out the two pattern pieces, indicating the overlap and fastener slits faintly with a pencil. Reinforce the back of each slit position with a tab of masking tape, then lay the two pieces flat, overlapping where indicated. Fix the pieces together with a strip of double-sided tape.

6 Make small slits where indicated on the template using a craft knife and cutting mat.

7 Cut an elongated triangular fastener from pine strip or thin card (cardboard) and insert into the slits.

8 Bend the lantern into a cylinder and fix the overlap with double-sided tape. Gently bend over the top of each petal shape.

CUT-OUT PAPER LANTERNS

These delicate handmade paper shades cast exquisite patterns of light through their Matisse-style cut-out designs. In the case of the triangular lantern, the shapes are only partly cut out so that the glow of the candle is cast upwards against the shade, creating a lovely play of light and shadow.

YOU WILL NEED
pastel-coloured handmade paper
pencil
ruler
scissors
tracing paper
craft knife and cutting mat
double-sided tape
kitchen knife

1 For the cylindrical lantern, scale up the template at the back of the book to fit a sheet of hand-made paper approximately 20 x 30 cm/8 x 12 in and transfer the motifs using tracing paper and a pencil.

2 Using a craft knife and a cutting mat, carefully cut around the traced outlines.

3 Place a strip of double-sided tape along one short side of the lantern and peel away the backing paper.

4 Curve the lantern to form a cylinder and press the overlap firmly together.

5 For the triangular lantern, scale up the template as before and trace the design lines on to a sheet of handmade paper. Using a craft knife and cutting mat, cut along the solid outlines only.

6 Lightly crease each motif along the dotted line so that the shapes protrude a little from the lantern.

7 On the reverse side of the paper, score along the vertical dotted fold lines using a ruler and the back of a kitchen knife.

8 Crease along the scored lines and bend the lantern into a triangular shape, fixing the overlap with a strip of double-sided tape.

MATERIALS

BEESWAX PELLETS

Beeswax is generally used in combination with other waxes to increase the burning time of a candle. It comes in subtle natural shades of yellow or brown or can be bleached white. It has a sticky quality so if more than 10% beeswax is being used for a moulded candle you should first use a releasing agent in the mould to prevent the candle from sticking.

BEESWAX SHEETS

These fine sweet-smelling sheets of wax are ideal for making rolled candles without using any heat source, though it may be helpful to warm the wax gently with a hairdryer if it is cold. Roll up the wax sheets around a piece of wick (See techniques).

CANDLE SCENTS

These are specially made in all kinds of fragrances to give candles an appealing scent as they burn. Usually in liquid form, a few drops are added to the molten wax mixture before dipping or moulding.

MOULD SEALER

This putty-like substance is used for making moulds watertight. It is easy to apply and remove and can be re-used over and over again.

PARAFFIN WAX

This generally comes in bead or pellet form and is the basic wax used for candle-making. It is a colourless, odourless product, which melts at a temperature between 40-71°C/104-160°F.

STEARIN

This is added to paraffin wax to increase its shrinking qualities, so that it acts as a releasing agent when making moulded candles. Stearin is added to the wax in a ratio of 1:10 - if you add too much the candle will have a soap-like appearance. Melt the stearin first, then add the wax dye, then the paraffin wax.

WAX DYE

Either in disc or powder form, wax dyes are added and dissolved in stearin. The amount of dye used will considerably alter the depth of colour obtained.

WAX GLUE

Available in block form, this soft, sticky wax is used to glue pieces of wax together and to stick decorations on to a candle. To use, melt a small amount in the top of a double boiler, and apply with a paintbrush.

WICKS

Wicks are made from braided cotton strands and come in varying thicknesses to suit the size of the candle. Wick sizes range from 1-10 cm/½-4 in. The measurement refers to the candle size, so you should use a 2.5 cm/1 in wick for a 2.5 cm/1 in diameter candle and so on. If the wick is too small, the flame will be too small. With the exception of dipped candles, the wick needs to be primed before you make the candle. To do this, melt a little paraffin wax in a double boiler. Leave the wicks to soak in the wax for a few minutes then remove the coated wicks. Lay them out straight on a baking tray lined with greaseproof paper and leave to harden.

WICK SUSTAINERS

These small metal discs are used to anchor the wick in container candles. The wick is pushed into the sustainer which sits flat on the base of the container.

Opposite, clockwise from left: wicks of different thicknesses; wax glue; primed wick; beeswax sheets; beeswax pellets; paraffin wax beads; stearin; mould sealer. From centre, clockwise from left: wax dyes; candle scents; wick sustainers.

EQUIPMENT

BAKING TRAY
An old baking tray is very useful for making sheets of wax and also as a base for candle moulds.

CRAFT KNIFE
You will need a sharp knife to cut wicks to length, to cut sheets of beeswax and to make stencils or templates for candles.

DIPPING CAN
This tall cylindrical can is used to hold liquid wax when making dipped candles. A large empty food can could also be used for this purpose. Stand the can in a pan of simmering water and do not allow to boil dry.

DOUBLE BOILER
This is an essential item for candle-making to prevent the molten wax from overheating and igniting. Ideally the boiler should be made of stainless steel or aluminium. Water is placed in the bottom pan and the wax melted in the top pan. Ensure the bottom pan does not boil dry by keeping it topped up with water.

GREASEPROOF PAPER
This is used as a liner when making sheets of wax or if melting down old wax.

MOULDS
These can be made from plastic, glass, rubber or metal and come in a wide variety of shapes and sizes. Care should be taken to wash and dry the moulds after use. Rubber and plastic moulds will not last as long as glass or metal moulds.

SPOONS
Use wooden spoons to mix the dye into the stearin and metal spoons for crushing dye discs.

WAX THERMOMETER
Always use a wax thermometer to ensure the wax is at the right temperature for each project. Never leave molten wax unattended and check the temperature regularly to prevent the wax from overheating.

WICKING NEEDLES
These needles come in various sizes and are used to insert wicks into candles as well as to support wicks at the top of moulds.

Opposite, clockwise from top left: greaseproof paper on baking tray; wax thermometer; wooden spoons; food can, to use as a dipping can; double boiler; craft knife; dipping can; metal pillar mould; wicking needles; plastic mould and base.

TECHNIQUES

Candle-making is a rewarding pastime and simple to learn. The techniques on the following pages will help you achieve beautiful and successful results at home.

CANDY-TWIST CANDLES

1 Adapt newly dipped candles while they are still malleable. On a clean, smooth surface, flatten the candle with a rolling pin until it is about 6 mm/¼ in thick. Avoid flattening the base of the candle as it will need to fit into a candleholder.

2 Begin twisting the candle by holding it near the wick between the thumb and forefinger of one hand and near the base with your other hand. Keep one hand steady and gently twist the candle with the other. You will need to work quickly while the wax is still warm.

3 Continue twisting the candle along its length. Check that the base will fit into a candleholder: if not, re-work it slightly with your fingers. Leave the candle to cool thoroughly.

ROLLED BEESWAX CANDLES

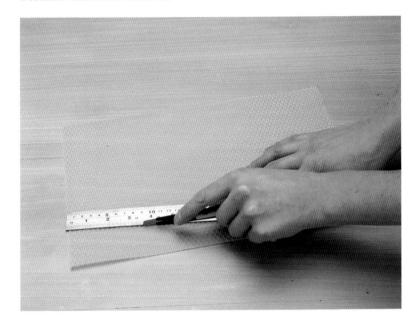

1 To make a tapered candle, use a rectangular sheet of beeswax. First warm the beeswax with a hairdryer. Using a craft knife and metal ruler, mark and cut off a narrow triangular segment from one of the long sides of the rectangle.

2 Cut a wick a few centimetres longer than the candle. Press the wick gently into the edge of the longer short side. Roll up the wax slowly and gently, checking that the wick is secured within the first turn.

3 Keep rolling the wax until you reach the opposite edge of the sheet. Press the edge into the candle to give a smooth finish.

4 Trim the wick, then wrap a tiny piece of beeswax around the wick to prime it ready for burning.

5 If you cut diagonally across a rectangular sheet of beeswax it will allow you to make a pair of tapered candles from one sheet.

ROLLED PILLAR CANDLE

BEEHIVE CANDLE

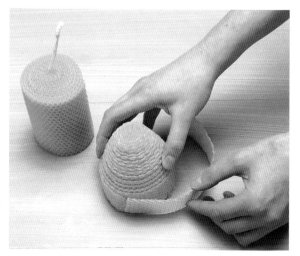

Roll sheets of beeswax around a wick and keep building up the layers until the candle is the required width. Join on extra sheets by butting the edges closely together.

To make a beehive candle, first roll a straight pillar candle around a wick, then build up the shape around this, adding bands of decreasing height.

TEMPLATES

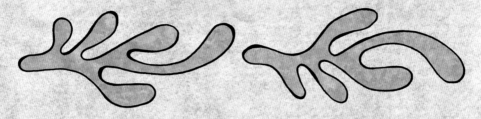

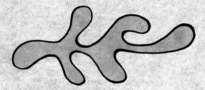

*Cut-out Paper Lanterns (cylindrical
lantern) pp 79-81 (reproduced 80%)*

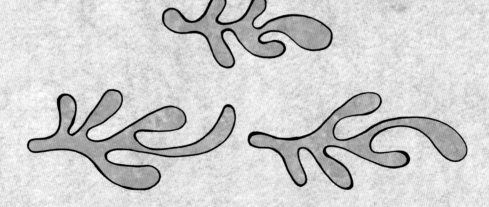

---

*Cut-out Paper Lanterns (triangular
lantern) pp 79-81 (reproduced 80%)*

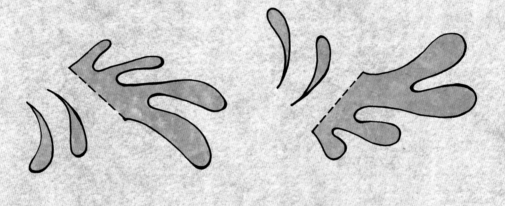

Rope Candlesticks
pp 72-75 (reproduced 73%)

Wire Candle Sconce pp 68-71
(reproduced 73%)

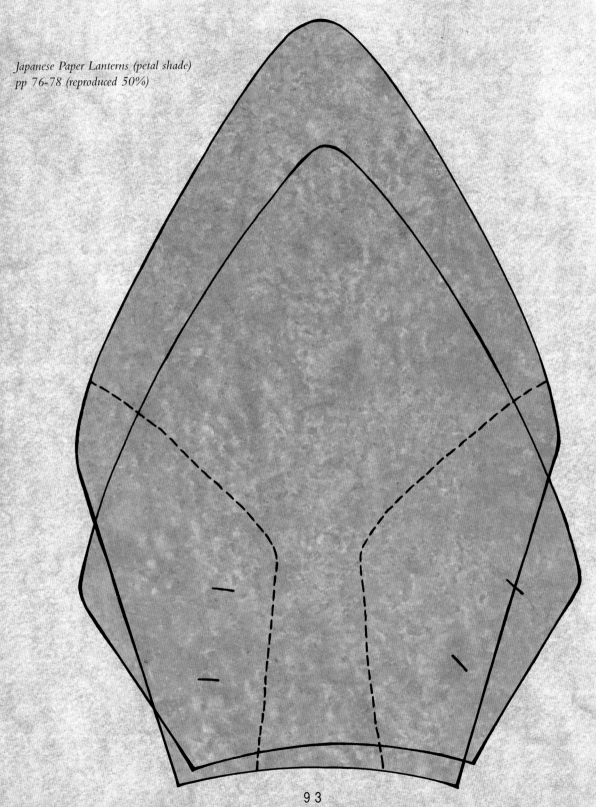

Japanese Paper Lanterns (petal shade)
pp 76-78 (reproduced 50%)

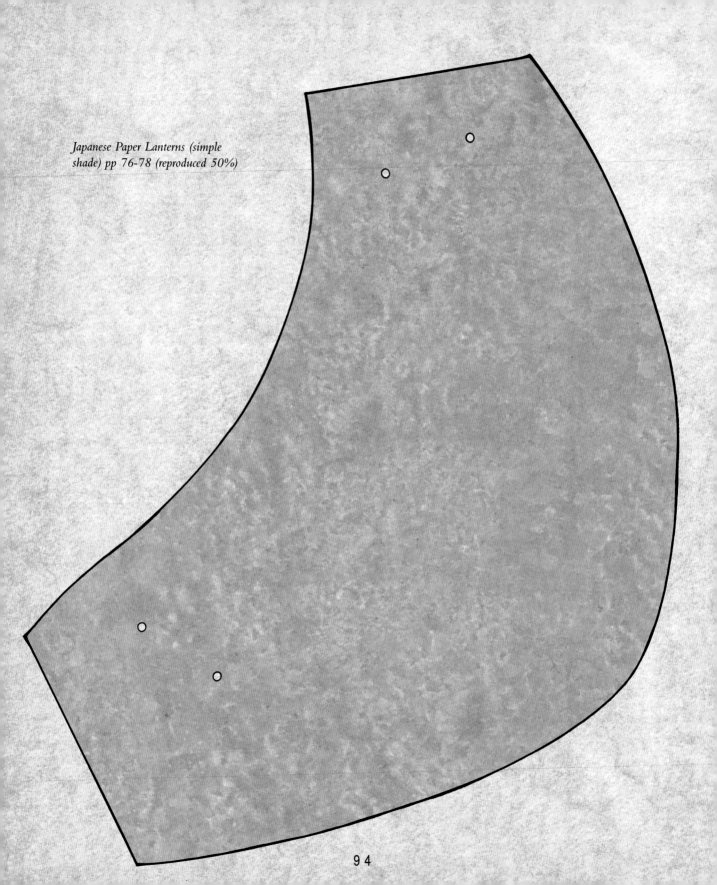

Japanese Paper Lanterns (simple shade) pp 76-78 (reproduced 50%)

STOCKISTS

United Kingdom
Angelic
6 Neal Street
London WC2H NLY
(0171) 240 2114
Candles and accessories

Candlemaker's Supplies
28 Blythe Road
London W14 0HA
(0171) 602 4031
Everything you will need to
make your own candles

Point à la Ligne
Michael Johnson (Ceramics) Ltd
81 Kingsgate Road
London NW6 4JY
(0171) 624 2493
Shaped candles, accessories and
modern ceramic candlesticks

United States
Barker Enterprises, Inc.
15106 10th Avenue, SW
Seattle, WA 98166
Candle supplies

Candlestick
2444 Broadway
New York, NY 10024
Candle supplies

Pottery Barn
Mail Order Department
P.O. Box 7044
San Francisco, CA 91420-7044

Canada
Charlotte Hobbys
782 Shield Road
Hemmingford
Quebec JOl 1HO
(516) 247 2590
Kits and candle supplies

Australia
The Craft Company
272 Victoria Avenue
Chatswood NSW 2067
(02) 413 1781
Waxes, wicks, dyes and moulds

Hornsby Beekeeping Supplies
63a Hunter Street
Hornsby NSW 2077
(02) 477 5569
Bulk and coloured wax and wicks

Janet's Art Supplies
145 Victoria Avenue
Chatswood NSW 2067
(02) 417 8572
Candle-making kits and beeswax

John L Guilfoyle Pty Ltd
772 Boundary Road
Darra QLD 4076
(07) 375 3677
Sheets of pure beeswax, sheets of
coloured beeswax, bulk beeswax
and candle wicks

also at:
23 Charles Street
St Mary's NSW 2670
(02) 623 5585

299 Prospect Road
Blair Athol SA 5084
(08) 344 8307

ACKNOWLEDGEMENTS

The author and publishers would like to thank the following for contributing
to this book: David Constable of The Candle Workshop, Gelligroes Mill,
Blackwood, Gwent for the Scented Candles, Dipped Candles, Sand Candles,
Carved Candles, Embossed Candles, Handmade Floating Candles and Cast
Candles. Alison Jenkins for the Rope Candlesticks, Wire Candle Sconce,
Japanese Paper Lanterns and Cut-out Paper Lanterns.

INDEX